WALKING IN HIS STEPS

HANDBOOK OF CHRISTIAN MINDFULNESS

DR. A. T. PRABHAKAR

INDIA • SINGAPORE • MALAYSIA

ISBN
Paperback 979-8-89588-372-3
Hardcase 979-8-89588-696-0

Contents

Introduction

In an age marked by constant distractions and unprecedented stress, the practice of mindfulness has emerged as a powerful tool for achieving mental clarity and emotional balance. Mindfulness, which involves paying full attention to the present moment with a non-judgmental attitude, has its roots in ancient contemplative traditions but has gained contemporary acclaim as a secular and scientific approach to mental health. Research has shown that mindfulness can reduce anxiety, depression, and stress while enhancing overall psychological well-being.

This handbook seeks to bridge the timeless wisdom of mindfulness with the rich spiritual heritage of Christianity. While mindfulness is often associated with eastern practices, its core principles are universal and can be harmoniously integrated into the Christian faith. Jesus Christ himself exemplified a life of profound presence, compassion, and mindfulness. By contemplating what Jesus would do in various contexts, we can draw closer to Him and enrich our spiritual and emotional lives.

Understanding Mindfulness

At its essence, mindfulness is the practice of being fully present in each moment. It involves observing our thoughts, emotions, and sensations without getting swept away by them or reacting impulsively. This awareness cultivates a deeper understanding of ourselves and our experiences, fostering a sense of inner peace and resilience.

Modern science supports the benefits of mindfulness. Studies have demonstrated that regular mindfulness practice can rewire the brain, improving areas related to attention, emotional regulation, and empathy. These findings have led to the widespread adoption of mindfulness techniques in therapeutic settings, educational institutions, and workplaces.

Mindfulness and Christian Faith

Incorporating mindfulness within the Christian faith does not mean adopting foreign beliefs but rather embracing a practice that complements and deepens our relationship with God. Jesus often withdrew to solitary places to pray and be still, embodying the very essence of mindfulness. By following His example, Christians can cultivate a mindful awareness that enhances their spiritual journey.

Mindfulness in a Christian context involves more than just personal well-being; it is about aligning our hearts and minds with God's will. Through mindful prayer, meditation on scripture, and living in the present moment, we can experience God's presence more fully and respond to His call with greater clarity and compassion.

The Christian view of Mindfulness

To incorporate mindfulness within a Christian context involves interpreting and integrating mindfulness practices through a Christian theological lens, bridging the gap between the contemplative practise and our spiritual needs. This begins with the understanding that mindfulness can be harmoniously aligned with Christian contemplative traditions, emphasizing the importance of being fully present with God. Mindfulness, in this sense, becomes a theological tool that enables Christians to cultivate a deeper awareness of God's omnipresence, to practice non-judgmental love and compassion, and to experience inner peace through active, present-cantered prayer and reflection. Christian mindfulness is grounded in the omnipresence of God. God Almighty is present "here, now, and forever," encompassing all spaces, including within our minds through the Holy Spirit. Jeremiah 23:24 and 1 Corinthians 6:19 affirm God's constant presence and the indwelling of the Holy Spirit in us. Mindfulness, when practiced with God's grace, helps to clear mental clutter—distractions, anxiety, and negative emotions—that obscure our awareness of God's presence. By calming the mind, Christians can create space for a deeper encounter with the Holy Spirit, as suggested by scriptures like Psalm 46:10 and Philippians 4:6-7. This practice enhances spiritual disciplines, making prayer, meditation, and contemplation more effective. Ultimately, mindfulness becomes a valuable tool that aligns with biblical teachings, allowing believers to experience God's guidance and presence more fully in their daily lives.

Psychological Benefits of Mindfulness

Mindfulness offers numerous psychological benefits:

- **Reduced Stress and Anxiety:** Mindfulness helps us manage stress by keeping our focus on the present moment rather than worrying about the past or future.

- **Enhanced Emotional Regulation:** By observing our emotions without immediate reaction, we gain better control over our responses, leading to healthier relationships and decision-making.

- **Increased Compassion and Empathy:** Mindfulness fosters a compassionate heart, enabling us to better love and serve others in the spirit of Christ.
- **Deeper Spiritual Connection:** Mindful practices can deepen our prayer life and help us to experience God's presence more intimately.
- As we embark on this journey of Christian mindfulness, let us walk in the steps of Jesus, embracing His teachings and example. Through mindful living, we can cultivate a more profound connection with God, enrich our spiritual lives, and enhance our overall well-being. This handbook will guide you through the principles and practices of Christian mindfulness, offering practical exercises and reflections to help you grow in faith.

Jeremiah 23:24
Can anyone hide himself in secret places,
So I shall not see him?" says the Lord;
"Do I not fill heaven and earth?" says the Lord.

1 Corinthians 6:19
Or do you not know that your body is the temple of the Holy Spirit who is in you, whom you have from God, and you are not your own?

Psalm 46:10
Be still, and know that I am God;
I will be exalted among the nations,
I will be exalted in the earth!

Philippians 4:6-7
Be anxious for nothing, but in everything by prayer and supplication, with thanksgiving, let your requests be made known to God; 7 and the peace of God, which surpasses all understanding, will guard your hearts and minds through Christ Jesus.

The Benefits of Mindfulness

Mindfulness helps in developing a well-balanced and insightful mind which is crucial for mental health and spiritual well-being. Modern psychology and neuroscience confirm the benefits of mindfulness practices, including reduced stress, improved emotional regulation, and enhanced cognitive functions. This chapter delves into these benefits from a Christian perspective, providing practical methods to cultivate such a mind, aligning with the teachings of Jesus and the values of the Christian faith.

The Psychological and Neuroscientific Perspective

Recent research in psychology and neuroscience has shown that mindfulness practices can lead to significant improvements in mental health. These practices help in:

1. **Reducing Stress**: Mindfulness helps reduce stress by alleviating anxiety and fostering a calm state of mind, which is reflected in lower cortisol levels. In Christian mindfulness, we can intentionally cast our anxieties onto God, staying present and finding peace, as encouraged in the Bible: "Cast all your anxiety on Him because He cares for you" (1 Peter 5:7).

2. **Improving Emotional Regulation**: By fostering awareness of one's emotions without judgment, mindfulness helps in managing emotional responses more effectively. This echoes the Christian virtue of self-control (Galatians 5:22-23).

3. **Enhancing Cognitive Functions**: Regular mindfulness practice has been shown to improve attention, memory, and executive functions, supporting overall cognitive health. A sound mind is crucial for discernment and wisdom (2 Timothy 1:7).

1 Peter 5:7
casting all your care upon Him, for He cares for you.

Galatians 5:22-23
But the fruit of the Spirit is love, joy, peace, longsuffering, kindness, goodness, faithfulness, gentleness, self-control. Against such there is no law.

2 Timothy 1:7
For God has not given us a spirit of fear, but of power and of love and of a sound mind.

Benefits of a Well-Balanced and Insightful Mind

A well-balanced and insightful mind brings numerous benefits, including:

1. **Emotional Stability**: Mindfulness helps in maintaining emotional equilibrium by reducing reactivity and promoting a balanced perspective on life's challenges. This stability reflects the peace of Christ that guards our hearts and minds (Philippians 4:7).

2. **Improved Relationships**: By cultivating empathy and compassion, mindfulness enhances interpersonal relationships and fosters a sense of connectedness. Loving our neighbours as ourselves (Mark 12:31) is facilitated through such mindful practices.

3. **Increased Resilience**: A mindful approach to life equips individuals with the tools to cope with stress and adversity more effectively. Trusting in God's strength (Philippians 4:13) and practicing mindfulness enhances our resilience.

4. **Enhanced Creativity**: A calm and clear mind is more open to creative insights and innovative solutions.

Practices for Cultivating a Well-Balanced and Insightful Mind

Mindful Breathing

Description: Mindful breathing is a fundamental practice in mindfulness that focuses on the breath as a way to anchor the mind in the present moment. This simple practice calms the mind and enhances present-moment awareness, creating space to connect with God.

Steps:

1. **Find a Quiet Space**: Sit comfortably in a quiet place where you won't be disturbed.
2. **Focus on Your Breath**: Close your eyes and bring your attention to your breath. Notice the sensation of the air entering and leaving your nostrils.
3. **Observe Each Inhale and Exhale**: Pay attention to each inhale and exhale, feeling the rise and fall of your chest or abdomen.

Philippians 4:7
and the peace of God, which surpasses all understanding, will guard your hearts and minds through Christ Jesus.

Mark 12:31
And the second, like it, is this: 'You shall love your neighbor as yourself.' There is no other commandment greater than these.

Philippians 4:13
I can do all things through Christ who strengthens me.

4. **Gently Redirect Your Focus**: If your mind wanders, gently bring your focus back to your breath without judgment. Offer a prayer of gratitude for this moment.

5. **Practice Regularly**: Start with a few minutes each day and gradually increase the duration as you become more comfortable with the practice.

Benefits:

- **Calms the Mind**: Reduces anxiety and stress by promoting relaxation, enabling a peaceful state to hear God's voice.
- **Enhances Present-Moment Awareness**: Cultivates a focused and attentive mind, reducing distractions and opening the heart to divine guidance.

Gratitude Journaling

Description: Gratitude journaling involves writing down things you are grateful for each day. This practice shifts focus towards positive experiences and cultivates a balanced mindset, echoing the biblical call to give thanks in all circumstances (1 Thessalonians 5:18).

> **1 Thessalonians 5:18**
> in everything give thanks; for this is the will of God in Christ Jesus for you.

Steps:

1. **Set Aside Time Each Day**: Choose a time, preferably in the morning or before bed, to reflect on your day.
2. **Write Down Three Things**: List three things you are grateful for. They can be simple, like a good meal, or profound, like the support of a loved one.
3. **Reflect on the Positive**: As you write, take a moment to reflect on why these things are meaningful to you and how they are blessings from God.
4. **Be Consistent**: Make this a daily habit to reinforce positive thinking and emotional balance.

Benefits:

- **Shifts Focus Towards Positivity**: Encourages a positive outlook by focusing on the good things in life, recognizing them as God's gifts.
- **Enhances Emotional Regulation**: Promotes feelings of happiness and contentment, counteracting negative emotions and fostering a heart of gratitude.

Integrating Mindfulness into Daily Life

To fully realize the benefits of a well-balanced and insightful mind, it is essential to integrate mindfulness practices into daily life. This involves not only setting aside time for formal practices like mindful breathing and gratitude journaling but also incorporating mindfulness into routine activities, seeing each moment as an opportunity to connect with God's presence.

Practical Tips:

- **Mindful Eating**: Pay full attention to the experience of eating, savoring each bite and noticing the flavors and textures. Give thanks for the provision of food.
- **Mindful Walking**: Walk slowly and mindfully, focusing on the sensations in your body and the environment around you, acknowledging the beauty of God's creation.
- **Mindful Listening**: When conversing with others, listen attentively without planning your response, truly hearing what the other person is saying, and showing Christ-like love and respect.

By embedding mindfulness in everyday activities, you cultivate a continuous state of awareness and insight that enriches all aspects of your life, helping you to live in a way that is attentive to God's guidance and presence.

Conclusion

Cultivating a well-balanced and insightful mind is a transformative journey that offers profound benefits for mental health and spiritual well-being. By practicing mindful breathing and gratitude journaling, you can develop a calm, focused, and positive mindset rooted in Christ's teachings. These practices provide a practical foundation for achieving a state of compassionate wisdom and inner peace, reflecting the mind of Christ in all you do.

Acknowledging and Letting Go of Unwholesome Thoughts and Deeds

Acknowledging and letting go of unwholesome thoughts and deeds is essential for mental clarity, emotional health, and spiritual growth. This process involves recognizing negative patterns and consciously choosing to release them, which can lead to a more peaceful and balanced mind. By addressing these thoughts and behaviours directly, we can prevent them from causing ongoing harm and cultivate a more positive and compassionate mindset. As Christians, we turn to God for forgiveness and strength, aligning our practices with His teachings and the example set by Jesus Christ, often asking, "What would Jesus do?"

The Importance of Acknowledgment and Release

Unwholesome thoughts and deeds, such as resentment, anger, guilt, and regret, can weigh heavily on the mind and heart. Holding onto these negative states not only impacts mental well-being but also affects physical health. By acknowledging these thoughts and choosing to let them go, we can break free from their grip and move towards a healthier state of mind, asking God for His forgiveness and healing. In every situation, we can contemplate, "What would Jesus do?" to guide our actions and thoughts.

Psychological and Spiritual Insights:

- **Emotional Cleansing**: Acknowledging and letting go of negative thoughts acts as an emotional cleanse, clearing out mental clutter and making room for positive emotions. This parallels the biblical concept of renewing our minds (Romans 12:2).
- **Reduction of Stress**: Letting go of unwholesome thoughts reduces the overall stress burden on the mind, contributing to a calmer and more relaxed state. "Cast all your anxiety on Him because He cares for you" (1 Peter 5:7).
- **Improved Relationships**: By releasing negative emotions such as resentment and anger, interpersonal relationships can improve, fostering greater understanding and compassion. "Be kind and compassionate to one another, forgiving each other, just as in Christ God forgave you" (Ephesians 4:32).

Practices for Acknowledging and Letting Go

Thought Observation

Description: Thought observation is a mindfulness practice where you sit quietly and observe your thoughts without judgment. This practice helps in recognizing negative or unwholesome thoughts and learning to let them go.

Steps:

1. **Find a Quiet Space**: Sit comfortably in a quiet place where you won't be disturbed.
2. **Settle into Stillness**: Close your eyes and take a few deep breaths to settle into stillness.
3. **Observe Your Thoughts**: Allow your thoughts to flow naturally. Observe them as they arise, without trying to change or judge them.
4. **Recognize Negative Patterns**: When you notice a negative or unwholesome thought, simply recognize it. Acknowledge its presence without attaching any judgment or emotion.
5. **Visualize Dissolution**: Visualize the negative thought dissolving away, like a cloud dispersing in the sky. Imagine it fading and leaving your mind clear. Pray for God's help in releasing these thoughts and ask yourself, "What would Jesus do?"
6. **Return to Breath**: If your mind wanders, gently bring your focus back to your breath, using it as an anchor.

Benefits:

- **Increases Awareness**: Enhances awareness of habitual thought patterns and helps in breaking the cycle of negativity.
- **Promotes Letting Go:** Encourages a healthy detachment from unwholesome thoughts, reducing their emotional impact.
- **Cultivates Mental Clarity**: Leads to a clearer and more focused mind, free from the clutter of negative thoughts.

Romans 12:2
And do not be conformed to this world, but be transformed by the renewing of your mind, that you may prove what is that good and acceptable and perfect will of God.

1 Peter 5:7
casting all your care upon Him, for He cares for you.

Ephesians 4:32
And be kind to one another, tenderhearted, forgiving one another, even as God in Christ forgave you.

Forgiveness Meditation

Description: Forgiveness meditation involves visualizing a person or situation you're holding resentment towards and consciously releasing that resentment, replacing it with compassion and understanding. This practice is deeply aligned with the Christian principle of forgiveness as taught by Jesus.

Steps:

1. **Find a Comfortable Position**: Sit comfortably in a quiet place where you can relax.
2. **Focus on Your Breath**: Close your eyes and take a few deep breaths to center yourself.
3. **Bring the Person/Situation to Mind**: Visualize the person or situation you're holding resentment towards. See them clearly in your mind.
4. **Acknowledge Your Feelings**: Recognize the feelings of resentment or anger you hold towards this person or situation. Allow yourself to fully feel these emotions without judgment.
5. **Begin the Release**: With each breath, imagine releasing a bit of the resentment. Visualize the negative emotions flowing out of you with each exhale. Ask God for the strength to forgive and let go.
6. **Replace with Compassion**: As you release resentment, consciously replace it with feelings of compassion and understanding. Imagine

sending kindness towards the person or situation, emulating Jesus' compassion.

7. **Affirm Forgiveness**: Silently affirm your intention to forgive, saying something like, "I choose to forgive and let go, as Christ has forgiven me."
8. **End with Gratitude**: Finish the meditation by expressing gratitude for the opportunity to release negativity and embrace compassion. Thank God for His forgiveness and grace.

Benefits:

- **Reduces Emotional Burden**: Helps in letting go of heavy emotions like anger and resentment, leading to emotional lightness.
- **Enhances Compassion**: Cultivates a sense of empathy and compassion towards others, improving relationships.
- **Promotes Inner Peace**: Leads to a deeper sense of inner peace and emotional balance.

Integrating Acknowledgment and Release into Daily Life

To make the practice of acknowledging and letting go a part of your daily life, consider incorporating mindfulness into routine activities and seeking God's guidance through prayer. Here are some practical tips:

Practical Tips:

- **Mindful Reflection**: Set aside a few minutes each day to reflect on your thoughts and emotions. Identify any negative patterns and practice letting them go, asking God for wisdom and strength. In challenging situations, pause and ask, "What would Jesus do?"
- **Daily Affirmations**: Use positive affirmations to reinforce your commitment to release unwholesome thoughts and embrace positivity. For example, "I let go of anger and embrace peace, through Christ who strengthens me."
- **Compassionate Interactions**: Practice forgiveness and compassion in your interactions with others. Approach conflicts with a mindset of understanding and empathy, following Jesus' example.

By regularly practicing these methods and seeking God's help, you can cultivate a habit of acknowledging and letting go of unwholesome thoughts and deeds, leading to a more balanced and peaceful state of mind.

Conclusion

Acknowledging and letting go of unwholesome thoughts and deeds is a crucial step towards mental clarity, emotional health, and spiritual growth. By incorporating practices such as thought observation and forgiveness meditation, and seeking God's forgiveness and strength, you can release negative patterns and cultivate a more positive and compassionate mindset. These practices not only enhance personal well-being but also improve relationships and foster a deeper sense of inner peace, reflecting the love and grace of Christ in your life. In every situation, ask yourself, "What would Jesus do?" and let His example guide your thoughts and actions.

Cultivation of Love and Compassion

Jesus is the embodiment of love and compassion, and His death on the cross for all humankind is the ultimate example of infinite love. Cultivating love and compassion is a transformative practice that opens the heart to the interconnectedness of all beings and fosters a deep sense of empathy and kindness. These qualities should become the foundational emotions guiding our interactions with the world. Love and compassion serve as the fertile ground from which mindfulness and wisdom can blossom. Thus, nurturing love and compassion is of paramount importance in our journey towards personal growth and societal harmony.

Understanding Compassion

Compassion arises as we recognize the shared experience of suffering among all beings. It becomes the lens through which we view the world, extending kindness and empathy to ourselves and others. Cultivating compassion means embracing the interconnectedness of all life forms and acknowledging the inherent worth and dignity present in each being. In Christianity, compassion is central to Jesus' teachings and actions. He consistently showed compassion to the suffering, the marginalized, and the outcast. By following His example, we can extend His love and kindness to others. The parable of the Good Samaritan (Luke 10:25-37) teaches us to show mercy and compassion to everyone, regardless of their background.

Importance of Compassion

In a world filled with challenges and uncertainties, compassion becomes our guiding light. It enriches our relationships, infuses our actions with meaning, and fosters a sense of unity and belonging. Compassion empowers us to navigate life's complexities with grace and resilience, bringing healing and solace to those in need. Jesus said, "Love your neighbour as yourself" (Mark 12:31). This commandment underscores the importance of compassion in our lives. By loving others as Jesus loves us, we can create a more compassionate and harmonious world. Jesus' own life was a testament to the transformative power of love and compassion.

Visualization of Jesus' Love

Visualizing Jesus' love on the cross and contemplating His ultimate act of forgiveness is a powerful meditation practice that can deepen our capacity for love and compassion. Here's a step-by-step guide to this meditation:

1. **Find a Quiet Space**: Choose a quiet and comfortable place where you won't be disturbed. Sit or lie down in a relaxed position.

2. **Settle into Stillness**: Close your eyes and take a few deep breaths to settle your mind and body. Allow yourself to become fully present in the moment.

3. **Visualize Jesus on the Cross**: Imagine Jesus on the cross, looking down with infinite love and compassion. See the pain and suffering He endured for the sake of humanity. Picture the scene vividly in your mind.

4. **Hear His Words of Forgiveness**: Visualize Jesus saying, "Father, forgive them, for they do not know what they are doing" (Luke 23:34). Feel the profound forgiveness and love in His words. Let this forgiveness wash over you, cleansing you of any resentment or bitterness.

5. **Reflect on His Love for His Disciples**: Imagine Jesus' immense love for His disciples, even as they forsook Him in His time of need. Reflect on the depth of His compassion and grace. Contemplate how He continued to love and forgive them.

6. **Apply Jesus' Love to Your Life**: Think about how you can embody Jesus' love and forgiveness in your everyday interactions. Consider situations where you can show compassion, understanding, and forgiveness. Ask yourself, "What would Jesus do?" and strive to respond with His love.

7. **End with Gratitude**: Conclude the meditation by expressing gratitude for Jesus' sacrifice and His infinite love. Thank Him for the strength and guidance to follow His example in your life.

By regularly practicing this visualization, you can deepen your understanding of Jesus' love and cultivate a more compassionate and forgiving heart.

Contemplation of the Good Samaritan

The parable of the Good Samaritan is a profound lesson in compassion and mercy. To internalize this teaching, engage in a contemplation meditation that allows you to experience both the vulnerability of the injured traveller and the compassion of the Samaritan.

Mark 12:31
And the second, like it, is this: 'You shall love your neighbor as yourself.' There is no other commandment greater than these.

Luke 23:34
Then Jesus said, "Father, forgive them, for they do not know what they do."

And they divided His garments and cast lots.

Step-by-Step Guide to the Good Samaritan Contemplation:

1. **Find a Comfortable Position**: Sit or lie down in a quiet place where you won't be disturbed. Close your eyes and take a few deep breaths to relax.

2. **Visualize the Traveller**: Imagine yourself as the traveller who was beaten and left by the roadside. Feel the pain, fear, and vulnerability of being in such a helpless situation. Reflect on your need for compassion and help.

3. **Feel the Desperation**: Allow yourself to deeply feel the desperation and hopelessness of the traveller. Recognize the human need for compassion and assistance.

4. **Visualize the Samaritan**: Now shift your perspective to that of the Good Samaritan. Imagine seeing the injured traveller and feeling a deep sense of compassion and empathy. Visualize yourself approaching the traveller, tending to their wounds, and providing comfort and assistance.

5. **Reflect on the Act of Kindness**: Contemplate the Samaritan's act of kindness and mercy. Consider the social and cultural barriers he overcame to help someone in need. Reflect on how this act embodies the teachings of Jesus.

6. **Apply to Your Life**: Think about situations in your life where you can act as the Good Samaritan. Identify opportunities to show kindness and compassion, even when it's challenging. Ask

yourself, "What would Jesus do?" in these situations and strive to follow His example.

7. **End with a Prayer**: Conclude the meditation with a prayer, asking God to help you embody the compassion and kindness of the Good Samaritan. Seek strength and guidance to act with love in all your interactions.

By engaging in this contemplation regularly, you can cultivate a deeper empathy for others and a stronger commitment to living out Jesus' teachings in your daily life.

Integrating Compassion into Daily Life

To fully integrate compassion into your daily life, consider incorporating these practices into routine activities and seeking God's guidance through prayer. Here are some practical tips:

Practical Tips:

- **Mindful Reflection**: Set aside a few minutes each day to reflect on your thoughts and emotions. Identify opportunities to show compassion and practice letting go of any judgments or negative feelings. In challenging situations, pause and ask, "What would Jesus do?"
- **Daily Affirmations**: Use positive affirmations to reinforce your commitment to cultivate compassion and love. For example, "I choose to love and show kindness, following Jesus' example."

- **Compassionate Interactions**: Practice forgiveness and compassion in your interactions with others. Approach conflicts with a mindset of understanding and empathy, following Jesus' teachings.

By regularly practicing these methods and seeking God's help, you can cultivate a habit of showing love and compassion, leading to a more balanced and peaceful state of mind.

Conclusion

Cultivating love and compassion is a crucial step towards personal growth, emotional health, and spiritual well-being. By incorporating practices such as the visualization of Jesus' love and the contemplation of the Good Samaritan, and seeking God's guidance, you can foster a more positive and empathetic mindset. These practices not only enhance personal well-being but also improve relationships and foster a deeper sense of inner peace, reflecting the love and grace of Christ in your life. In every situation, ask yourself, "What would Jesus do?" and let His example guide your thoughts and actions.

Getting rid of Distractions

Being constantly aware of the mind's susceptibility to distraction is essential for inner wellbeing. Distractions can manifest in various forms, including pride, greed, hatred, and lust, which are common struggles for many individuals. In the Christian tradition, these distractions are viewed as obstacles to spiritual growth and alignment with God's will.

Pride:

Pride, often characterized by an inflated sense of self-importance or superiority, can lead to arrogance and a lack of humility. Jesus, however, exemplified humility throughout His life, despite being the Son of God. He washed His disciples' feet, a task typically reserved for servants, demonstrating that true greatness lies in serving others (John 13:1-17). When faced with prideful thoughts or behaviours, Christians can emulate Jesus by practicing humility and putting the needs of others above their own.

Exercise: Mindfulness of Pride

Sit comfortably in a quiet space and take a few deep breaths to centre yourself. Allow your mind to settle, and observe your thoughts as they arise.

Notice if the word "I" predominates in your thoughts, signalling a focus on self-importance or superiority. Pay attention to any feelings of pride that may arise, such as a desire for recognition or a sense of entitlement.

Visualize the scene from John 13:1-17 where Jesus humbly washes His disciples' feet. Picture the humility and love reflected in His actions, despite His divine status as the Son of God. Allow this image to sink in and resonate with you.

Contemplate on how Jesus must have felt in that moment – the humility, compassion, and selflessness He demonstrated towards His disciples. Reflect on

His willingness to serve others, even in positions of authority, as a model of true greatness.

Cultivate humility in your own heart by acknowledging your limitations and weaknesses. Recognize that true greatness lies not in exalting oneself but in serving others with love and compassion. Pray for God's grace to help you embody humility in your thoughts, words, and actions.

Commit to practicing humility in your daily life, seeking opportunities to serve others and put their needs above your own. Allow the example of Jesus washing His disciples' feet to inspire and guide you in your journey towards humility and selflessness.

Greed:

Greed, the insatiable desire for wealth or material possessions, can foster selfishness and disregard for others. Jesus warned against the dangers of greed, emphasizing the importance of prioritizing spiritual wealth over material riches (Luke 12:15). In the parable of the rich fool, Jesus condemned the accumulation of wealth for selfish gain, highlighting the transient nature of earthly possessions (Luke 12:13-21). When confronted with greed, Christians can follow Jesus' example by prioritizing generosity and stewardship, using their resources to bless others rather than hoarding them for personal gain.

Exercise: Mindfulness of Greed

Find a quiet and comfortable space to sit in a relaxed posture, allowing your body to unwind and your mind to settle. Take a few deep breaths, focusing on the sensation of the breath entering and leaving your body.

Reflect on any desires or cravings you may have for wealth or material possessions. Notice if there is a sense of attachment or insatiability associated with these desires.

Recall the teachings of Jesus regarding greed, particularly His warning in Luke 12:15 about the dangers of prioritizing earthly wealth over spiritual richness. Consider the parable of the rich fool in Luke 12:13-21, where Jesus condemns the accumulation of wealth for selfish gain.

Visualize the scene from the parable, imagining the rich man who hoarded his abundant harvest for himself, only to lose his life that very night. Reflect on the fleeting nature of earthly possessions and the folly of placing one's hope and security in material wealth.

Contemplate on Jesus' call to prioritize generosity and stewardship over greed and selfishness. Ponder on ways you can use your resources to bless others and advance God's kingdom on earth.

Pray for guidance and strength to resist the temptations of greed and to cultivate a generous and compassionate heart. Ask God to help you align your priorities with His kingdom values, seeking first His righteousness and trusting in His provision.

Commit to practicing generosity and stewardship in your daily life, seeking opportunities to share your blessings with those in need and to use your resources for the greater good. Let the example of Jesus' teachings on greed inspire and motivate you to live a life marked by generosity, contentment, and faithfulness.

Hatred:

Hatred, characterized by intense hostility or aversion towards others, can poison relationships and hinder forgiveness. Jesus taught the importance of love and forgiveness, even towards enemies. He instructed His followers to love their enemies and pray for those who mistreated them (Matthew 5:44). When faced with feelings of hatred or resentment, we can embody Jesus' teachings by extending grace and compassion to those who have wronged them, seeking reconciliation and peace rather than retaliation.

Exercise: Mindfulness of Hatred

Find a quiet and peaceful space where you can sit comfortably without distractions. Close your eyes and take several deep breaths, allowing your body and mind to relax.

Bring to mind any feelings of anger, resentment, or hatred that you may be holding towards someone. Notice the sensations and emotions associated with these feelings, without judgment or condemnation.

Reflect on the teachings of Jesus regarding hatred and forgiveness, particularly His command to love our enemies and pray for those who mistreat us (Matthew 5:44). Consider the radical nature of this command and its implications for how we relate to others.

As you continue your contemplation, visualize Jesus standing before you, radiating with compassion and grace. See His gentle demeanour and the warmth in His eyes as He extends His hand towards you.

Now, imagine yourself in a situation where someone has wronged you, perhaps insulted you or treated you unfairly. Feel the surge of anger or resentment rising within you as you recall the hurtful words or actions.

In this moment, envision Jesus standing beside you, His presence calming your agitated emotions. See Him turning the other cheek in response to the offense, embodying the teachings He shared during His earthly ministry.

As you witness this act of humility and non-retaliation, allow yourself to feel the weight of His example. Notice how His actions speak volumes about the transformative power of love and forgiveness, even in the face of injustice.

Reflect on the profound courage and strength it takes to follow Jesus' example of turning the other cheek, especially in situations where retaliation may seem justified. Consider the impact of responding with grace and compassion, rather than perpetuating a cycle of conflict and animosity.

With Jesus as your guide and inspiration, commit to embodying His teachings of love and forgiveness in your own life. Visualize yourself following His example, extending grace and compassion towards those who wrong you, and embracing the transformative power of non-violence and reconciliation.

As you conclude your contemplation, offer a prayer of surrender and commitment to God, asking for His guidance and strength to live out Jesus' teachings in your daily interactions. Trust in His grace to empower you to turn the other cheek and respond with love, even in the face of adversity.

Lust:

Lust, the intense desire for sexual gratification outside the bounds of God's design, can lead to objectification and exploitation of others. Jesus emphasized the sanctity of marriage and the importance of purity in thought and action (Matthew 5:27-30). He urged His followers to guard their hearts against lustful desires, recognizing that indulging in such desires can lead to sin. When confronted with lustful temptations, Christians can follow Jesus' example by practicing self-discipline and honouring God's design for sexuality, seeking fulfilment within the context of committed, loving relationships.

In each of these situations, Christians can look to Jesus as the ultimate example of how to overcome distractions and live according to God's will. By following His teachings and emulating His character, believers can navigate the challenges of pride, greed, hatred, and lust with wisdom, grace, and integrity.

Exercise: Mindfulness of Lust

Reflect on Jesus' teachings regarding purity of heart and the sanctity of marriage. Recall His words from Matthew 5:27-30, where He emphasized the importance of guarding against lustful desires and honouring God's design for sexuality.

As you meditate on these teachings, consider the consequences of indulging in lustful thoughts and actions. Reflect on how such behaviour can lead to objectification and exploitation of others, dishonouring both God and fellow human beings.

Now, imagine yourself surrendering these lustful desires to Jesus, placing them at His feet with sincerity and humility. Feel His presence surrounding you, offering you strength and grace to resist temptation and live according to His will.

Commit yourself to practicing self-discipline and honouring God's design for sexuality in your thoughts, words, and actions. Seek fulfilment within the context of committed, loving relationships, recognizing that true intimacy and satisfaction are found in alignment with God's plan.

As you conclude your contemplation, offer a prayer of surrender and dedication to God, asking for His continued guidance and support in overcoming lustful temptations. Trust in His grace to empower you to live a life of purity and integrity, following Jesus' example with wisdom and humility.

Conclude in Prayer

Conclude your contemplation by offering a prayer of surrender to God. Thank Him for His grace and ask for His guidance in overcoming distractions and living according to His will. Commit yourself to seeking God's kingdom above all else and to following Jesus' example of humility, generosity, love, and purity. Surrender your desires, fears, and struggles to God, trusting in His faithfulness to lead and empower you. Ask for the strength to resist temptation and to live a life that honors and glorifies God in every thought, word, and deed.

Building Patience

Patience is a fundamental virtue that fosters mental peace and resilience in the face of challenges. Cultivating patience allows us to navigate life's complexities with equanimity and grace, leading to greater fulfilment and success in achieving our long-term goals. Patience finds profound significance in the teachings of Jesus Christ. His life exemplified patience in its truest form, from enduring trials and persecution to demonstrating unwavering trust in God's timing and plan. As followers of Christ, we are called to emulate His patience and resilience in our own lives, trusting that God's timing is perfect and His plans are for our ultimate good (Romans 8:28). In the practice of patience, Christians can find solace and guidance in the example set by Jesus during His earthly ministry. His interactions with people, His response to adversity, and His teachings all reflect a patient and compassionate spirit that we are encouraged to embody in our daily lives.

The Importance of Patience

Patience is not merely the ability to wait; it's the capacity to maintain a sense of inner calm and composure amidst adversity. By cultivating patience, we develop resilience, emotional stability, and a deeper understanding of ourselves and the world around us.

Exercise in Practice

Description: Choose a task that inherently requires patience, such as assembling a puzzle or engaging in a detailed project. Approach the task with mindfulness, observing any feelings of impatience that arise and gently redirecting your focus back to the present moment.

Steps:

1. **Select a Task:** Choose an activity that demands patience and sustained attention, such as solving a puzzle, painting, or engaging in a creative endeavour.

> **Romans 8:28**
>
> And we know that all things work together for good to those who love God, to those who are the called according to His purpose.

2. **Practice Mindfulness:** Begin the task with a clear intention to cultivate patience. Notice any impulses or desires for quick results that arise within you.

3. **Observe Impatience:** As you engage in the activity, observe any feelings of impatience that arise. Notice the sensations in your body and the thoughts in your mind without judgment.

4. **Gently Redirect Focus:** Whenever you notice impatience creeping in, gently redirect your focus back to the task at hand. Bring your attention to the present moment and the process of engaging with the activity.

5. **Repeat Practice:** Continue engaging in the task mindfully, repeating the process of observing impatience and gently redirecting your focus as needed.

Exercise: Contemplation on Christ's Patience

Visualize the scene from the Garden of Gethsemane (Matthew 26:36-46), where Jesus grapples with the impending agony of his crucifixion. In this moment, Jesus demonstrates profound patience and submission to God's will, despite the immense suffering he knows awaits him.

Imagine Jesus, in deep anguish, praying fervently to God, "My Father, if it is possible, may this cup be taken from me. Yet not as I will, but as you will." Visualize him wrestling with the weight of his impending sacrifice, yet ultimately surrendering to God's plan with unwavering patience and trust.

See Jesus' disciples sleeping nearby, unable to fully comprehend the gravity of the situation. Despite feeling abandoned by his closest friends, Jesus remains steadfast in his resolve to fulfill his divine purpose.

As you reflect on this scene, consider the depth of Jesus' patience and obedience in the face of unimaginable suffering. Draw inspiration from his example of unwavering faith and trust in God's plan, even when it requires enduring great trials and tribulations.

Through this exercise, we not only develop our capacity for patience but also deepen our connection to the teachings and example of Jesus, finding inspiration and guidance in His timeless wisdom.

Keeping the Zeal

Maintaining enthusiasm and zeal is essential for maintaining wellbeing. It involves finding joy and purpose in everyday activities, cultivating a sense of passion and dedication that sustains us through life's challenges. To infuse the practices for cultivating zeal and enthusiasm with Christian principles, let's integrate teachings from the Bible and offer exercises inspired by the Christian faith:

1. Embracing the Joys of Everyday Life:

- Reflect on the biblical passage from Psalm 118:24, which says, "This is the day that the Lord has made; let us rejoice and be glad in it." Recognize that each day is a gift from God, filled with opportunities for gratitude and joy.

- Start each day with a prayer of thanksgiving, expressing gratitude to God for the blessings of life. Throughout the day, pause to acknowledge God's presence in the beauty of nature, the kindness of others, and the moments of joy that unfold.

2. Engaging in Hobbies:

- Consider the parable of the talents (Matthew 25:14-30), where Jesus encourages faithful stewardship of the gifts and abilities entrusted to us. Recognize that pursuing our passions can be a form of honouring and multiplying the talents God has given us.
- Reflect on your talents and interests, considering how you can use them to glorify God and serve others. Dedicate time each week to engage in activities that align with your passions, offering them as acts of worship and service to God.

3. Nature Reflection:

- Spend time in nature, observing God's creation with mindful awareness. As you take in the beauty of the natural world, reflect on the Creator behind

Psalm 118:24

This is the day the Lord has made;
We will rejoice and be glad in it.

it all and offer gratitude for His handiwork. Allow the sights, sounds, and smells of nature to awaken your senses and deepen your appreciation for God's presence in every aspect of your life.

4. Worship Music:

- Listen to worshipful music that uplifts your spirit and draws your focus towards God. Allow the melodies and lyrics to wash over you, stirring your soul with praise and adoration. Sing along or simply listen with a receptive heart, allowing the music to create a sacred space for communion with God.

By integrating Christian teachings into our practices, we can cultivate a joyous and enthusiastic spirit rooted in faith and gratitude. As we embrace the joys of everyday life and engage in activities that reflect our deepest passions, may we be inspired by the love of Christ and empowered by His Spirit to live with zeal and enthusiasm for His glory.

Meditative Concentration

Meditative concentration, serves as a powerful tool for deepening one's connection with God and nurturing spiritual growth. By directing the mind's attention to God's presence and teachings, individuals can cultivate inner peace, clarity, and a profound sense of communion with the Divine.

The Significance of Meditative Concentration

In Christian meditation, the focus is not on emptying the mind but on filling it with thoughts of God's love, wisdom, and presence. Meditative concentration enables believers to quiet the noise of the world and center their attention on God, fostering a deeper relationship with Him and a greater awareness of His guidance in their lives.

Practices for Cultivating Meditative Concentration

1. **Breath Awareness:** Begin by finding a comfortable seated position and gently closing your eyes. Direct your attention to the sensation of your breath as it flows in and out of your body. With each inhale, contemplate God's life-giving presence filling you with His Spirit, and with each exhale, release any worries or distractions into His care.

2. **Scripture Meditation:** Choose a passage from the Bible that resonates with you and spend time meditating on its meaning and significance. As you read the passage, reflect on how God's words apply to your life and invite His presence to illuminate your understanding.

3. **Contemplative Prayer**: Engage in contemplative prayer by silently repeating a prayer or sacred phrase that reflects your desire to draw closer to God. Allow the words to sink deep into your heart, guiding your thoughts and intentions towards God's will and purpose for your life.

4. **Visualization:** Practice imaginative prayer by visualizing scenes from the life of Jesus or moments from the Bible. Enter into the story with all your senses, imagining yourself walking alongside Jesus or witnessing His miracles first-hand. Allow the Holy Spirit to speak to you through your imagination, revealing insights and truths about God's character and love.

Through these practices of meditative concentration, Christians can nurture a deeper awareness of God's presence, wisdom, and love in their lives, leading to greater spiritual growth, inner peace, and communion with the Divine.

Cultivating Wisdom

In the Christian faith, transcending conceptual thinking involves aligning our minds with the wisdom and guidance of God, moving beyond rigid thought patterns to embrace His divine truth and love. This wisdom is essential for deepening our faith and understanding, as it allows us to let go of attachments to worldly ideas and concepts, and to embrace the transformative power of God's grace in our lives

The Transient Nature of worldly Phenomena:

As Christians, we understand that life is a continual procession of change, guided by the sovereign hand of God. Phenomena arise and pass away according to His divine will, reflecting the impermanence and transience that pervades all of creation. Mountains rise and fall, rivers ebb and flow, and seasons transition in accordance with God's divine timing. Even our thoughts, emotions, and sensations are subject to His divine providence, arising and passing away according to His greater purpose for our lives. This transient nature of all phenomena serves as a reminder of the temporal nature of earthly existence and the eternal nature of God's kingdom.

Wonder and Inter-being of all God's creation

Within the intricate tapestry of God's creation, everything is intimately connected and interdependent, reflecting His divine wisdom and providence. As human beings created in His image, we exist as a complex web of relationships, bound together by His love and grace. Every aspect of our existence, from the beating of our hearts to the breath in our lungs, is sustained by His divine power and mercy. Just as the body relies on its various organs and systems to function harmoniously, so too are we reliant on one another for support, guidance, and fellowship in our journey of faith. In recognizing the interdependence and interbeing that define our relationship with God and one another, we cultivate a deeper sense of gratitude, humility, and reverence for His divine creation.

Exercise: Contemplating the Transfiguration

1. **Find a Quiet Space**: Begin by finding a quiet and peaceful space where you can engage in contemplative prayer without distractions. This

could be a quiet room in your home, a serene outdoor setting, or a sacred space in your place of worship.

2. **Settle into a Comfortable Position:** Sit comfortably in a chair or cushion with your back straight and your hands resting gently on your lap. Close your eyes or keep them softly focused on a focal point in front of you.

3. **Deep Breathing**: Take a few deep breaths to centre yourself and quiet your mind. Inhale slowly and deeply through your nose, allowing your abdomen to expand fully. Exhale slowly and completely through your mouth, releasing any tension or stress with each breath.

4. **Visualize the Scene**: In your mind's eye, imagine yourself on the mountain with Jesus, Peter, James, and John. Picture the radiant light emanating from Jesus, illuminating His face and clothing. See Moses and Elijah standing beside Him, conversing with Him.

5. **Listen to the Divine Voice**: As you visualize the scene, listen attentively to the voice from heaven declaring, "This is my Son, whom I love; with him I am well pleased. Listen to him!" Allow these words to resonate deeply within you, reminding you of Jesus' divine identity and the Father's love for His Son.

6. **Reflect on Jesus' Compassion**: Contemplate the profound love and compassion that Jesus demonstrated throughout His ministry on earth. Reflect on His healing touch, His words of comfort,

and His willingness to embrace the marginalized and the suffering. Consider how His divine nature was revealed in His acts of mercy and grace.

7. **Contemplate Jesus' Sacrifice:** Consider the significance of Jesus willingly leaving the mountaintop, where He was glorified, to descend into the valley of human suffering. Reflect on His ultimate act of love and sacrifice, knowing that He chose to endure the agony of the cross for the redemption of humanity.

8. **Personal Application:** Take a moment to consider how the Transfiguration and Jesus' sacrificial love speak to your own life and faith journey. How does Jesus' divine and compassionate nature inspire you to live with greater love, compassion, and service towards others? How can you embody the spirit of the Transfiguration and Jesus' sacrifice in your daily life?

9. **Prayer and Gratitude:** Conclude your contemplation with a prayer of gratitude for the revelation of Jesus' divine glory, His compassionate presence in your life, and His sacrificial love. Offer thanks for the opportunity to deepen your understanding of the Transfiguration and ask for guidance in living out its lessons in your life.

10. **Practice Regularly:** Consider incorporating this exercise into your spiritual practice on a regular basis, allowing the insights and revelations of the Transfiguration and Jesus' sacrifice to deepen and enrich your relationship with God and your journey of faith.

Way Forward in Everyday Life

As we embark on the journey forward, let's explore how we can integrate mindfulness, love, compassion, patience, zeal, and wisdom into our everyday lives, drawing inspiration from the teachings of Jesus Christ.

Mindfulness: Practice being fully present in each moment, just as Jesus was attentive to the needs of those around Him. Take time to quiet your mind, listen to your thoughts, and engage with the world around you with intentionality. Contemplate on a verse from the Bible, such as Philippians 4:8, "Finally, brothers and sisters, whatever is true, whatever is noble, whatever is right, whatever is pure, whatever is lovely, whatever is admirable—if anything is excellent or praiseworthy—think about such things." Reflect on what Jesus would do in each moment, focusing your mind on thoughts that align with God's truth and goodness.

Love and Compassion: Embody the love and compassion that Jesus demonstrated throughout His ministry. Treat others with kindness, empathy, and forgiveness, regardless of their circumstances. Contemplate on a scene from the Bible, such as the story of the Good Samaritan (Luke 10:25-37), and reflect on what Jesus would do in showing love and compassion to those in need.

Avoiding Distractions: Stay focused on your spiritual journey, resisting the distractions of the world that pull you away from God. Set aside time for prayer, meditation, and Scripture reading, prioritizing your relationship with Christ above all else. Contemplate on a verse from the Bible, such as Matthew 6:33, "But seek first his kingdom and his righteousness, and all these things will be given to you as well." Reflect on what Jesus would do in staying centered on His mission and purpose, even amidst worldly distractions.

Building Patience: Cultivate patience in the face of life's challenges, trusting in God's timing and sovereignty. Practice patience in your interactions with others, responding with grace and understanding even in difficult situations. Contemplate on a verse from the Bible, such as James 1:3-4, " knowing that the testing of your faith produces patience. But let patience have *its* perfect work, that you may be perfect and complete, lacking nothing.." Reflect on what Jesus would do in demonstrating patience and endurance, trusting in His Father's plan.

Keeping Zeal: Maintain enthusiasm and passion for serving God and others, following the example of Jesus' fervent devotion to His Father's will. Channel your energy into activities that glorify God and further His kingdom on earth. Contemplate on a scene from the Bible, such as Jesus cleansing the temple (Matthew 21:12-13), and reflect on what Jesus would do in pursuing righteousness with zeal and commitment.

Cultivating Wisdom: Seek wisdom from God through prayer, Scripture study, and seeking counsel from mature believers. Allow God's Word to guide your thoughts, decisions, and actions, leading you on the path of righteousness. Contemplate on a verse from the Bible, such as Proverbs 3:5-6, "Trust in the Lord with all your heart and lean not on your own understanding; in all your ways submit to him, and he will make your paths straight." Reflect on what Jesus would do in seeking divine wisdom and discernment, surrendering to His Father's guidance.

In embracing mindfulness, love, compassion, patience, zeal, and wisdom, and contemplating what Jesus would do in each aspect of our lives, we can walk confidently on the path of faith, following in the footsteps of our Savior and Lord.

Matthew 21:12-13

Then Jesus went into the temple of God and drove out all those who bought and sold in the temple, and overturned the tables of the money changers and the seats of those who sold doves. 13 And He said to them, "It is written, 'My house shall be called a house of prayer,' but you have made it a 'den of thieves.

As we integrate these principles into our daily lives and contemplate what Jesus would do in each situation, we find ourselves walking in closer fellowship with our Saviour, experiencing His presence and guidance in all aspects of our journey. May we continue to grow in faith, love, and obedience, striving to live out the teachings of Jesus Christ in every thought, word, and deed. And may our lives be a testimony to His grace, mercy, and transforming power, drawing others into the abundant life found only in Him.

Luke 10:25-37

And behold, a certain [a]lawyer stood up and tested Him, saying, "Teacher, what shall I do to inherit eternal life?"

26 He said to him, "What is written in the law? What is your reading of it?"

27 So he answered and said, " 'You shall love the Lord your God with all your heart, with all your soul, with all your strength, and with all your mind,' and 'your neighbor as yourself.' "

28 And He said to him, "You have answered rightly; do this and you will live."

29 But he, wanting to justify himself, said to Jesus, "And who is my neighbor?"

30 Then Jesus answered and said: "A certain man went down from
Jerusalem to Jericho, and fell among [b]thieves, who stripped him of his
clothing, wounded him, and departed, leaving him half dead. 31 Now by
chance a certain priest came down that road. And when he saw him, he
passed by on the other side. 32 Likewise a Levite, when he arrived at the
place, came and looked, and passed by on the other side. 33 But a certain
Samaritan, as he journeyed, came where he was. And when he saw him,
he had compassion. 34 So he went to him and bandaged his wounds,
pouring on oil and wine; and he set him on his own animal, brought him
to an inn, and took care of him. 35 On the next day, [c]when he departed,
he took out two denarii, gave them to the innkeeper, and said to him,
'Take care of him; and whatever more you spend, when I come again, I
will repay you.' 36 So which of these three do you think was neighbor to
him who fell among the thieves?"

37 And he said, "He who showed mercy on him."

Then Jesus said to him, "Go and do likewise."

Luke 12:13-21

Then one from the crowd said to Him, "Teacher, tell my brother to divide the inheritance with me."

14 But He said to him, "Man, who made Me a judge or an arbitrator over you?" 15 And He said to them, "Take heed and beware of [a]covetousness, for one's life does not consist in the abundance of the things he possesses."

16 Then He spoke a parable to them, saying: "The ground of a certain rich man yielded plentifully. 17 And he thought within himself, saying, 'What shall I do, since I have no room to store my crops?' 18 So he said, 'I will do this: I will pull down my barns and build greater, and there I will store all my crops and my goods. 19 And I will say to my soul, "Soul, you have many goods laid up for many years; take your ease; eat, drink, and be merry."' 20 But God said to him, 'Fool! This night your soul will be required of you; then whose will those things be which you have provided?'

21 "So is he who lays up treasure for himself, and is not rich toward God.

John 13:1-17

Now before the Feast of the Passover, when Jesus knew that His hour had come that He should depart from this world to the Father, having loved His own who were in the world, He loved them to the end.

2 And [a]supper being ended, the devil having already put it into the heart of Judas Iscariot, Simon's son, to betray Him, 3 Jesus, knowing that the Father had given all things into His hands, and that He had come from God and was going to God, 4 rose from supper and laid aside His garments, took a towel and girded Himself. 5 After that, He poured water into a basin and began to wash the disciples' feet, and to wipe them with the towel with which He was girded. 6 Then He came to Simon Peter. And Peter said to Him, "Lord, are You washing my feet?"

7 Jesus answered and said to him, "What I am doing you do not understand now, but you will know after this."

8 Peter said to Him, "You shall never wash my feet!"

Jesus answered him, "If I do not wash you, you have no part with Me."

9 Simon Peter said to Him, "Lord, not my feet only, but also my hands and my head!"

10 Jesus said to him, "He who is bathed needs only to wash his feet, but is completely clean; and you are clean, but not all of you." 11 For He knew who would betray Him; therefore He said, "You are not all clean."

12 So when He had washed their feet, taken His garments, and sat down again, He said to them, "Do you [b]know what I have done to you? 13 You call Me Teacher and Lord, and you say well, for so I am. 14 If I then, your Lord and Teacher, have washed your feet, you also ought to wash one another's feet. 15 For I have given you an example, that you should do as I have done to you. 16 Most assuredly, I say to you, a servant is not greater than his master; nor is he who is sent greater than he who sent him. 17 If you know these things, blessed are you if you do them.

Luke 10:25-37

And behold, a certain [a]lawyer stood up and tested Him, saying, "Teacher, what shall I do to inherit eternal life?"

26 He said to him, "What is written in the law? What is your reading of it?"

27 So he answered and said, " 'You shall love the Lord your God with all your heart, with all your soul, with all your strength, and with all your mind,' and 'your neighbor as yourself.' "

28 And He said to him, "You have answered rightly; do this and you will live."

29 But he, wanting to justify himself, said to Jesus, "And who is my neighbor?"

30 Then Jesus answered and said: "A certain man went down from
Jerusalem to Jericho, and fell among [b]thieves, who stripped him of his
clothing, wounded him, and departed, leaving him half dead. 31 Now by
chance a certain priest came down that road. And when he saw him, he
passed by on the other side. 32 Likewise a Levite, when he arrived at the
place, came and looked, and passed by on the other side. 33 But a certain
Samaritan, as he journeyed, came where he was. And when he saw him,
he had compassion. 34 So he went to him and bandaged his wounds,
pouring on oil and wine; and he set him on his own animal, brought him
to an inn, and took care of him. 35 On the next day, [c]when he departed,
he took out two denarii, gave them to the innkeeper, and said to him,
'Take care of him; and whatever more you spend, when I come again, I
will repay you.' 36 So which of these three do you think was neighbor to
him who fell among the thieves?"

37 And he said, "He who showed mercy on him."

Then Jesus said to him, "Go and do likewise."

Matthew 25:14-30

"For the kingdom of heaven is like a man traveling to a far country, who
called his own servants and delivered his goods to them. 15 And to
one he gave five talents, to another two, and to another one, to each
according to his own ability; and immediately he went on a journey. 16
Then he who had received the five talents went and traded with them,
and made another five talents. 17 And likewise he who had received two
gained two more also. 18 But he who had received one went and dug
in the ground, and hid his lord's money. 19 After a long time the lord of
those servants came and settled accounts with them.

20 "So he who had received five talents came and brought five other
talents, saying, 'Lord, you delivered to me five talents; look, I have gained
five more talents besides them.' 21 His lord said to him, 'Well done, good
and faithful servant; you were faithful over a few things, I will make you
ruler over many things. Enter into the joy of your lord.' 22 He also who
had received two talents came and said, 'Lord, you delivered to me two
talents; look, I have gained two more talents besides them.' 23 His lord
said to him, 'Well done, good and faithful servant; you have been faithful
over a few things, I will make you ruler over many things. Enter into the
joy of your lord.'

24 "Then he who had received the one talent came and said, 'Lord, I knew
you to be a hard man, reaping where you have not sown, and gathering
where you have not scattered seed. 25 And I was afraid, and went and hid
your talent in the ground. Look, there you have what is yours.'

26 "But his lord answered and said to him, 'You wicked and lazy servant,
you knew that I reap where I have not sown, and gather where I have
not scattered seed. 27 So you ought to have deposited my money with
the bankers, and at my coming I would have received back my own with
interest. 28 So take the talent from him, and give it to him who has ten
talents.

29 'For to everyone who has, more will be given, and he will have
abundance; but from him who does not have, even what he has will be
taken away. 30 And cast the unprofitable servant into the outer darkness.
There will be weeping and gnashing of teeth.'

Matthew 26:36-46

Then Jesus came with them to a place called Gethsemane, and said
to the disciples, "Sit here while I go and pray over there." 37 And He
took with Him Peter and the two sons of Zebedee, and He began to be
sorrowful and deeply distressed. 38 Then He said to them, "My soul is
exceedingly sorrowful, even to death. Stay here and watch with Me."

39 He went a little farther and fell on His face, and prayed, saying, "O My
Father, if it is possible, let this cup pass from Me; nevertheless, not as I will,
but as You will."

40 Then He came to the disciples and found them sleeping, and said to Peter,
"What! Could you not watch with Me one hour? 41 Watch and pray, lest you
enter into temptation. The spirit indeed is willing, but the flesh is weak."

42 Again, a second time, He went away and prayed, saying, "O My Father,
[a]if this cup cannot pass away from Me unless I drink it, Your will be done."
43 And He came and found them asleep again, for their eyes were heavy.

44 So He left them, went away again, and prayed the third time, saying
the same words. 45 Then He came to His disciples and said to them, "Are
you still sleeping and resting? Behold, the hour [b]is at hand, and the
Son of Man is being betrayed into the hands of sinners. 46 Rise, let us be
going. See, My betrayer is at hand."

Mindfulness schedule

Morning Routine **Before Starting the Day (15 minutes):** • Begin with 5 minutes of prayer, offering thanks for the gift of a new day and asking for guidance and strength. • Transition into 5 minutes of mindful prayer, focusing on your breath and cultivating awareness of the present moment. • Spend the remaining 5 minutes reflecting on a passage from the Bible related to love, compassion, or kindness towards oneself and others.
Midday Pause **Midday Break (5 minutes):** • Take a short 5-minute break to pause and reconnect with God. Offer a brief prayer of gratitude for the blessings of the day so far and ask for continued guidance and presence.
Nightly Routine: **Before Bed (15 minutes):** • Start with reading a passage of scripture or a devotional that brings comfort and peace. • Transition into 5 minutes of mindful prayer, focusing on your breath and cultivating love and compassion in present moment. • Conclude with a 5-minute prayer of surrender, entrusting yourself and your worries to God's care and embracing His peace as you prepare for restful sleep.

www.ingramcontent.com/pod-product-compliance
Lightning Source LLC
LaVergne TN
LVHW021144160826
845679LV00023B/2044

9798895883723